YOUR KNOWLEDGE HAS VALUE

R.W. Hndoosh, M.S. Saroa, S. Kumar

Modelling of an Interval Type-2 Fussy Logic System (IT2 FLS) on Continuous Domain with Medical Application

GRIN Publishing

Bibliographic information published by the German National Library:

The German National Library lists this publication in the National Bibliography; detailed bibliographic data are available on the Internet at http://dnb.dnb.de .

Imprint:

Copyright © 2015 GRIN Verlag GmbH
Print and binding: Books on Demand GmbH, Norderstedt Germany
ISBN: 978-3-656-94228-3

GRIN - Your knowledge has value

Since its foundation in 1998, GRIN has specialized in publishing academic texts by students, college teachers and other academics as e-book and printed book. The website www.grin.com is an ideal platform for presenting term papers, final papers, scientific essays, dissertations and specialist books.

Visit us on the internet:

http://www.grin.com/

http://www.facebook.com/grincom

http://www.twitter.com/grin_com

IOSR Journal of Computer Engineering (IOSR-JCE)
e-ISSN: 2278-0661,p-ISSN: 2278-8727,
PP 45-57
www.iosrjournals.org

Modelling of an IT2 FS on Continuous Domain with Medical Application

Rana Waleed Hndoosh[1], M. S. Saroa[2], Sanjeev Kumar[3]

[1](Dept. of Software Engineering, College of Computers Sciences & Mathematics, Musol. University, Iraq
[2](Dept. of Mathematics, Maharishi Markandeshawar University, Mullana-133207, India
[3](Dept. of Mathematics, IBS College, Dr. B. R. Ambedkar University, Khandari Campus, Agra-282002, India

Abstract—*An overview and a derivation of interval type-2 fussy logic system (IT2 FLS), which can handle rule's uncertainties on continuous domain, having good number of applications in real world. This work focused on the performance of an IT2 FLS that involves the operations of a fuzzification, inference, and output processing. The output processing consists of Type-Reduction (TR) and defuzzification. This work made IT2 FLS much more accessible to FLS modellers, because it provides mathematical formulation for calculating the derivatives. Presenting extend to representation of T2 FSs on continuous domain and using it to derive formulas for operations, we developed and extended the derivation of the union of two IT2 FSs to the derivation of the intersection and union of N-IT2 FSs that is based on various concepts. The derivation of all the formulas that are related with an IT2 and these formulas depend on continuous domain with multiple rules. Each rule has multiple antecedents that are activated by a crisp number with T2 singleton fuzzification (SF). Then, we have shown how those results can be extended to T2 non-singleton fuzzification (NSF). We are derived the relationship between the consequent and the domain of uncertainty (DOU) of the T2 fired output FS. As well as, provide the derivation of the general form at continuous domain to calculate the different kinds of type-reduced. We have also applied an IT2 FLS to medical application of Heart Diseases (HDs) and an IT2 provide rather modest performance improvements over the T1 predictor. Finally, we made a comparison of HDs result between IT2 FLS using the IT2FLS in MATLAB and the IT2 FLS in Visual C# models with T1 FISs (Mamdani, and Takagi-Sugeno).*

Keywords—*Type-1 fuzzy logic system, Type-2 fuzzy sets, Type-2 fuzzy logic system, Type-2 membership functions, Interval type-2 fuzzy systems, Footprint of uncertainties, Type-reduction, Data base of Heart diseases.*

1. INTRODUCTION

This work, introduced a new class of fuzzy logic systems—*interval type-2 fuzzy logic system* (IT2 FLS), where the antecedent or/and consequent membership functions (MFs) are interval type-2 fuzzy sets (IT2 FSs), [10-14], which is an extension of the concept of a *type-1 fuzzy set* (T1 FS). In an IT2 FLS, the knowledge used to construct rules is uncertain, and this uncertainty drives to rules having uncertain antecedents and/or consequents, [21-23]. Now as MFs of a general T2 FSs are fuzzy, therefore T2 FSs are able to model as uncertainties, and their MFs are three-dimensional, [24]. T2 FSs third dimension provides additional degrees that make it possible to directly models uncertainties, [8]. T2 FSs are difficult to use and understand because: i) T2 FSs three-dimensional makes them very difficult to depict; ii) there is no simple terms set that let us effective communication about T2 FSs, and to then be mathematically accurate, and iii) using T2 FSs is computationally more complex than using T1 FSs, [10-13], [17]. Most people only use an IT2 FSs in a T2 FLS, because of the computational complex of using a general T2 FS, the result being an IT2 FLS. The resulting IT2 FLS have the chance to provide better performance than a T1 FLS, and all of the results that are needed to perform an IT2 FLS can be obtained by T1 FS mathematics. The computations related with IT2 FSs are very flexible, which makes an IT2 FLS to a large degree practical, [16]. Section 2, defined a small set of concepts in a mathematically accurate way of general T2 FSs and IT2 FSs. We are extended the theorem1, which was given by Mendel et al. 2006 for discrete universes of discourse, to continuous universes of discourse. Section 3, derived the formulas of the *intersection* and *union* of N-IT2 FSs that is based on different concepts: i) the concept of embedded IT2 FSs such as Theorem 3.1; ii) the concept of *Extension Principle* such as Theorem 3.2. Additionally, we derived the formulas of the *meet* and *join* of N-IT2 FSs such as Theorem 3.3, [4-7]. Section 4 has described an IT2 FLS, T2 singleton fuzzification (SF) and T2 non-singleton fuzzification (NSF). Present the derivation of all of the formulas that are related with an IT2 FLS at continuous domain, and handled multiple rules. Each rule has multiple antecedents that are activated by a crisp number (the case of SF), after which we shown how those results can be extended to (the case of NSF), [11-15]. Consequently, we are derived the relationship between the consequent and the domain of uncertainty (DOU) of the T2 fired output FS that summarized by Theorem 4.1 and 4.2 for SF and NSF, respectively, [1]. Section 5, showed that computation of the con-

IOSR Journal of Computer Engineering (IOSR-JCE)
e-ISSN: 2278-0661,p-ISSN: 2278-8727,
PP 45-57
www.iosrjournals.org

tinuous version of type-reduction that is used in going from fired-rule IT2 FSs to the defuzzified number at the final output of FLS, [20], [4], [6]. We have provided the derivation of the general form for continuous domain to calculate the different kinds of type-reduced, which was given by Karnik et al. 2004 but for discrete domain. Additionally, we are presented the term of defuzzification which using the average of endpoints to obtain the crisp output of IT2 FLS, [10], [12], [13], [18]. In Section 6, a medical application of IT2 FLS's to heart diseases (HDs) is applied, which demonstrated the basic ideas and the mathematical operations of IT2 fuzzy sets and systems. We also provide a Matlab performance of IT2 FLS. A comparison of HDs between IT2 FLS using the IT2FLS in MATLAB and the IT2FLS in Visual C# models with T1 FISs (Mamdani, and Takagi-Sugeno) are presented in this Section. Section 7, we draw conclusions. Finally, an Appendix is presents the concept of Extension Principle.

2. INTERVAL TYPE-2 FUZZY SETS

Most people only use interval type-2 fuzzy sets (IT2 FSs) in a type-2 fuzzy logic system (T2 FLS) because of the computational complexity of using a general T2 FS, the result being an interval type-2 fuzzy logic system (IT2 FLS). We define an IT2 FS and some important related concepts, to provide a simple collection of mathematically terms that will let us effectively communicate about such sets. Imagine fuzzing the type-1 membership function (MF) depicted through Fig. 1(a) by moving the points on the trapezoid either to the right or to the left with the different amounts, as in Fig. 1(b). Therefore, at a specific value of x, say x' for all $x \in X$, there no longer is a single value for the MF; instead, the MF takes on values wherever the vertical line intersects the fuzzy. The basic concepts of type-2 fuzzy sets are introduced at an Appendix A, [11-13], [17].

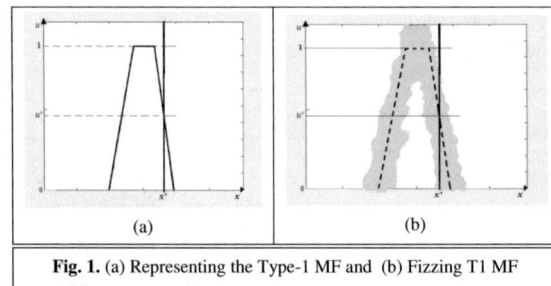

	(a)		(b)

Fig. 1. (a) Representing the Type-1 MF and (b) Fizzing T1 MF

Theorem 2.1: Let $\hat{A}_E^k$ denote the kth embedded IT2 FSs for T2 FS, when X and U are continuous, is as follows:

$$\hat{A}_E^k \equiv \left\{ \left(u_i^k, \mu_{\hat{A}}(x_i, u_i^k) \right), i = 1, \dots, \infty \right\}, \tag{1}$$

where $u_i^k \in \{u_{ij}, j = 1, \dots, M_i\}$, then $\hat{A}$ is the union of all of its embedded IT2 FSs, i.e,

$$\hat{A} = \int_{k=1}^{n_{N \to \infty}} \hat{A}_E^k \tag{2}$$

in which $n_{N \to \infty} \equiv \prod_{i=1}^{\infty} M_i$, and M_i denotes the partition levels of secondary variable u_i^k at each of the x_i.

3. SET-THEORETIC OPERATIONS ON TYPE-2 FUZZY SETS

The main aim of this section is to derive formulas for the *intersection* and *union* of N IT2 FSs of an IT2 FS, because these operations are used in an IT2 FLS. In this Section, the derivation of the *intersection* and *union* of N IT2 FSs is based on tow concepts: 1) the concept of embedded IT2 FSs such as theorem 2.1; 2) the concept of *Extension Principle* such as theorem 3. Third part contains the derivation of the *meet* and *join* of N IT2 FSs, [4-7] [10], [12], [17].

Theorem 3.1: Derivation the intersection of N-T2 FSs depending on the concept of the embedded IT2 FSs

The *intersection* and *union* of N IT2 FSs, $\hat{A}_i$ ($i = 1, \dots, N$) are given by (3) and (4), respectively:

$$\bigcap_{i=1}^{N} \hat{A}_i = 1 / \left[\bigwedge_{i=1}^{N} \underline{\mu}_{\hat{A}_i}(x), \bigwedge_{i=1}^{N} \overline{\mu}_{\hat{A}_i}(x) \right], \forall x \in X. \tag{3}$$

IOSR Journal of Computer Engineering (IOSR-JCE)
e-ISSN: 2278-0661,p-ISSN: 2278-8727,
PP 45-57
www.iosrjournals.org

$$\bigcup_{i=1}^{N} \hat{A}_i = 1 / \left[\bigvee_{i=1}^{N} \underline{\mu}_{\hat{A}_i}(x), \bigvee_{i=1}^{N} \overline{\mu}_{\hat{A}_i}(x) \right], \forall \, x \in X. \tag{4}$$

Theorem 3.2: Derivation the intersection of N-T2 FSs depending on the concept of the Extension Principle
Let $\hat{A}_i$ T2 FSs in a continuous universe X_c. Suppose $\mu_{\hat{A}_i}(x) = \int_u g_{ix}(u_i)/u_i$, $(i = 1, \ldots, N)$ and $\forall \, x \in X_c$ be the membership degrees of $\hat{A}_i$, where $u_i \in J_x^u$. Then membership degrees for intersection and union of type-2 FS have been defined as follows:

$$\bigcap_{i=1}^{N} \hat{A}_i \Leftrightarrow \mu_{\hat{A}_1 \cap \ldots \cap \hat{A}_N}(x) = \int_{u_1 \in J_x^u} \cdots \int_{u_N \in J_x^u} \left(g_{1x}(u_1) \star \ldots \star g_{Nx}(u_N) \right) / T(u_1 \star \ldots \star u_N) \tag{5}$$

$$\bigcup_{i=1}^{N} \hat{A}_i \Leftrightarrow \mu_{\hat{A}_1 \cup \ldots \cup \hat{A}_N}(x) = \int_{u_1 \in J_x^u} \cdots \int_{u_N \in J_x^u} \left(g_{1x}(u_1) \star \ldots \star g_{Nx}(u_N) \right) / T(u_1 \vee \ldots \vee u_N) \tag{6}$$

Theorem 3.3: Derivation the meet operations of N-T2 FSs depending on the concept of the secondary MF
Suppose that we have n convex, normal, type-1 real fuzzy sets $\hat{A}_i$ described by membership functions a_i respectively.
Let x_i be real numbers such that $x_1 \leq x_2 \leq \cdots \leq x_n$ and $a_1(x_1) \leq \cdots \leq a_n(x_n)$, then,

$$\mu_{A_1 \cap \ldots \cap A_n}(\alpha) = \bigcap_{i=1}^{N} \hat{A}_i = \begin{cases} \bigvee_{i=1}^{n} a_i(\alpha), & \alpha < x_1 \\ \bigwedge_{i=1}^{k} a_i(\alpha), & x_k \leq \alpha < x_{k+1}, 1 \leq k < n - 1 \\ \bigwedge_{i=1}^{n} a_i(\alpha), & \alpha \geq x_n \end{cases} \tag{7}$$

4. INTERVAL TYPE-2 FUZZY LOGIC SYSTEM

We assume that all the antecedent and consequent fuzzy sets in the rules are T2. A FLS is T2 as long as any one of its antecedent or consequent FSs is T2. The rules structure remains the same in the case of T2, but some or all of the FSs involved are T2, [16], [24]. The T2 FLS has n inputs $x_1 \in X_1, \ldots, x_n \in X_n$, and output $y \in Y$, and, is describe by L rules, where the lth rule has the form

$$R^l : \text{if } x_1 \text{ is } \hat{A}_1^l \text{ and } \ldots \text{ and } x_n \text{ is } \hat{A}_n^l \text{ then } y \text{ is } \hat{B}^l, \quad l = 1, \ldots, L. \tag{8}$$

If all of the antecedent and consequent T2 FSs are IT2 FSs, then we call the resulting T2 FLS an IT2 FLS. A rule-base contains four components: rules, fuzzifier, inference system, and output processing that consist of defuzzifier and type-reducer. The outputs of the T2 FLS are the type-reduced set and the crisp defuzzified value, [11], [13], [17].

4.1. Type-2 Singleton Fuzzification Model

From the rule (8), let $\hat{A}_1^l, \hat{A}_2^l, \ldots, \hat{A}_n^l$ be IT2 FSs in continuous universe of discourses $X_{1c}, X_{2c}, \ldots, X_{nc}$, respectively, and $\hat{B}^l$ be an IT2 FS in continuous universe of discourse Y_c. Decompose each $\hat{A}_i^l$ into its $n_{A_i} \to \infty$ $(i = 1, \ldots, n)$ embedded IT2 FSs $\hat{A}_{i_E}^{ki^l}$, as the following:

$$\hat{A}_i^l = \int_{ki=1}^{n_{A_i}} A_{i_E}^{ki^l} = 1/\text{DOU}\left(\hat{A}_i^l\right), \quad i = 1, \ldots, n., \tag{9}$$

where

$$\text{DOU}\left(\hat{A}_i^l\right) = \int_{ki=1}^{n_{A_i}} A_{i_E}^{ki^l} = \int_{ki=1}^{n_{A_i}} \int_{j=1}^{N_{x_i} \to \infty} u_{ij}^{ki}/x_{ij}, \quad u_{ij}^{ki} \in J_{x_{ij}} \subseteq [0,1]. \tag{10}$$

We also decompose $\hat{B}^l$ into $n_B \to \infty$ embedded IT2 FSs $\hat{B}_E^{k^l}$, whose domains are the embedded T1 FSs $B_E^{k^l}$; we see that $\hat{B}^l$ can be expressed as:

IOSR Journal of Computer Engineering (IOSR-JCE)
e-ISSN: 2278-0661,p-ISSN: 2278-8727,
PP 45-57
www.iosrjournals.org

$$\hat{B}^l = \int\limits_{k=1}^{n_B \to \infty} \hat{B}_E^{k^l} = 1/DOU(\hat{B}^l) \tag{11}$$

where

$$DOU(\hat{B}^l) = \int\limits_{k=1}^{n_B \to \infty} B_E^{k^l} = \int\limits_{k=1}^{n_B \to \infty} \int\limits_{j=1}^{N_y \to \infty} v_j^k / y_j, \quad v_j^k \in J_{y_j} \subseteq [0,1] \tag{12}$$

Cartesian product of antecedents $\hat{A}_1^{\ l} \times \dots \times \hat{A}_n^{\ l}$ has $\left(\prod_{i=1}^n n_{A_i}\right) \to \infty$ collections of the embedded T1 FSs $A_{i_E}^{ki^l}$. The relationship between $\hat{A}_i^{\ l}$ antecedents and consequent $\hat{B}^l$ can be represented by:

$$\mu_{\hat{A}_1^l \to B^l}(x, y) = \mu_{\hat{A}_1^l \times \dots \times \hat{A}_n^{\ l} \to B^l}(x, y) = \mu_{\hat{A}_1^l \times \dots \times \hat{A}_n^{\ l}}(x) + \mu_{B^l}(y)$$

$$= \mu_{\hat{A}_1^{\ l}}(x_1) + \dots + \mu_{\hat{A}_n^{\ l}}(x_n) + \mu_{B^l}(y) = \left[S_{i=1}^n \mu_{\hat{A}_i^{\ l}}(x_i) \right] + \mu_{B^l}(y), \tag{13}$$

where it has been supposed that Mamdani implications are used, multiple antecedents are connected by *or* (i.e. by S-norms), S is short for an S-norm and $+$ represents the max S-norms, [24].

In general, there are L rules that describe an IT2 FLS and repeatedly more than one rule fires when input is applied to that system. Consequently, we have $n_{A_1} \times \dots \times n_{A_n} \times n_B$ collections of embedded T1 antecedent and consequent FSs, which generate all fired output sets for all collections of antecedent and consequent FSs, as the following [10], [12], and [18]:

$$D^l(y) = \int\limits_{k1=1}^{n_{A_1} \to \infty} \dots \int\limits_{kn=1}^{n_{A_n} \to \infty} \int\limits_{k=1}^{n_B \to \infty} \mu_{D^l(k1,\dots,kn,k)}(y), \quad \forall y \in Y_c \tag{14}$$

The relationship between the consequent $D^l(y)$ in (14) and the DOU of the T2 fired output FS is made a summary by theorem 5a, [21-23].

Theorem 4.1: The output $D^l(y)$ in (14) that calculated by using T1 FS is the same as the DOU of the T2 fired output FS, which is calculated by using T2 FS.

4.2. Type-2 Non-singleton Fuzzification Model

Let the n-dimensional input is given by the IT2 FS, and we suppose $\hat{X}_i$ denote the IT2 FSs describing each of the n inputs. More specifically $\hat{X}_1, \hat{X}_2, \dots, \hat{X}_n$ are IT2 FSs in continuous universes of discourse $X_{1c}, X_{2c}, \dots, X_{nc}$. There are L rules that described an IT2 FLS, and repeatedly more than one rule fires when input is applied to that system. Decompose $\hat{A}_i$ into their $n_{X_i} \to \infty$ ($i = 1, \dots, n$) embedded IT2 FSs $\hat{X}_{i_E}^{hi}$, i.e., [1], [11], [13], [17]

$$\hat{X}_i = \int\limits_{hi=1}^{n_{X_i} \to \infty} \hat{X}_{i_E}^{hi}, \quad i = 1, \dots, n. \tag{15}$$

The domain of each $\hat{X}_{i_E}^{hi}$ is the embedded T1 FS $X_{i_E}^{hi}$. The Cartesian product be $\hat{X}_1 \times \hat{X}_2 \times \dots \times \hat{X}_n$, has $\left(\prod_{i=1}^n n_{X_i}\right) \to \infty$ collections of the embedded T1 FSs $X_{i_E}^{hi}$, then the MF of a fuzzy Cartesian product is given by:

$$\mu_{X_1}(x_1) + \dots + \mu_{X_n}(x_1) = S_{i=1}^n \mu_{X_i}(x_i) \tag{16}$$

Since, each rule determines a fuzzy set D in Y such that when we use Zadeh's sup-star composition, note that:

$$\mu_{D^l}(y) = \sup_{x, x_i \in X_c} \left[\left(\mu_{X_1}(x_1) + \dots + \mu_{X_n}(x_n) \right) + \mu_{\hat{A}_i^l \to B^l}(x, y) \right], \quad y \in Y$$

$$= \sup_{x, x_i \in X_c} \left[S_{i=1}^n \mu_{X_i}(x_i) + S_{i=1}^n \mu_{\hat{A}_i^{\ l}}(x_i) + \mu_{B^l}(y) \right] = \sup_{x, x_i \in X_c} \left\{ \left[S_{i=1}^n \mu_{X_i}(x_i) + \mu_{\hat{A}_i^{\ l}}(x_i) \right] + \mu_{B^l}(y) \right\} \tag{17}$$

Then, we have derived the formula of *NSF* as the following:

IOSR Journal of Computer Engineering (IOSR-JCE)
e-ISSN: 2278-0661,p-ISSN: 2278-8727,
PP 45-57
www.iosrjournals.org

$$\mu_{D^l}(y) = \left[S_{i=1}^n \left(\sup_{x_i \in X_{ic}} \mu_{X_i}(x_i) \dotplus \mu_{\tilde{A}_i^l}(x_i) \right) \right] \dotplus \mu_{B^l}(y), \quad \forall \, y \in Y_c \tag{18}$$

Since, there are $n_B \to \infty$ embedded T1 FSs for the consequent, $\left(n_A = \prod_{i=1}^n n_{A_i}\right) \to \infty$ embedded T1 FSs for the antecedents, $\left(n_X = \prod_{i=1}^n n_{X_i}\right) \to \infty$ embedded T1 FSs for the inputs; then, we obtain $\left(n_{X_1} \times ... \times n_{X_n} \times n_{A_1} \times .. \times n_{A_n} \times n_B\right)$ collections of input, antecedent, and consequent embedded T1 FSs as shown in Figure. 4, which generate $\mu_{D^l}(y)$ as the following, [9], [14], [15]:

$$\mu_{D^l}(y) = \int_{h_1=1}^{n_{X_1} \to \infty} \cdots \int_{h_n=1}^{n_{X_n} \to \infty} \int_{k_1=1}^{n_{A_1} \to \infty} \cdots \int_{k_n=1}^{n_{A_n} \to \infty} \int_{k=1}^{n_B \to \infty} \mu_{D^l(h_1,...,h_n,k_1...,k_n,k)}(y) \tag{19}$$

In order to represent the structure of $\mu_{D^l}(y)$ using network, we depict (19) through Fig. 4, for a *single-antecedent rule*.

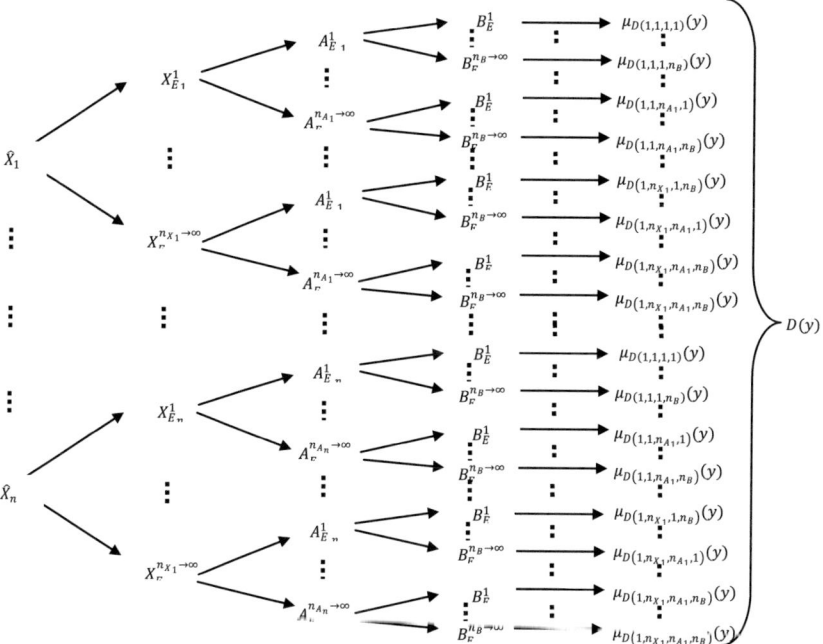

Fig. 4: Fired output FSs $\forall \, n_D = n_X \times n_A \times n_B$ collections of the embedded T1 antecedent and consequent FSs for N antecedent rules

Theorem 4.2: The output $D^l(y)$ in (19), calculated by using T1 FS is the same as the DOU of the T2 fired output FS, which is calculated by using T2 FS.

5. THE OUTPUT PROCESSING

Type-Reduction (TR) is a first step of output processing, in order to compute the centroid of an IT2 FS. We are derived to compute the centroid of an IT2 FS because when all sources of uncertainty disappear, the IT2 FLS must reduce to a T1 FLS. We define the centroid ($C_{\tilde{D}}$) of an IT2 FS $\tilde{D}$ such as the set of all of the centroids of all of its embedded IT2 FSs. depend on (18) and (19) note that, we must compute the centroid of all of the $n_D \to \infty$ embedded T1 FSs contained within $\mathrm{DOU}(\tilde{D}^l)$. Therefore, we obtain a set of n_D numbers that have both a minimum and maximum element,

IOSR Journal of Computer Engineering (IOSR-JCE)
e-ISSN: 2278-0661,p-ISSN: 2278-8727,
PP 45-57
www.iosrjournals.org

$c_l(\hat{D}) \equiv c_l$ and $c_r(\hat{D}) \equiv c_r$, respectively. The centroid of each of the embedded T1 FSs is a limited number. Related with each of these numbers will be a membership degree of one as the following, [4-5], [21-23], and [20]:

$$C_{\bar{D}} = 1/[c_l(\hat{D}), c_r(\hat{D})]$$

The generalized centroid $[c_l(\hat{D}), c_r(\hat{D})]$ is a closed interval, c_l and c_r can be computed from the lower and upper MF of $\hat{A}$ as follows:

$$c_l(\hat{D}) = min \text{ \{centroid of all embedded T1 FSs in DOU}(\hat{D})\} = min_{l \in R}\left(C(A_{E_l})\right)$$

$$c_l(\hat{D}) = \min_{l \in R}\left(\frac{\int_1^\infty x\,\mu_{A_{E_l}}(x)\,dx}{\int_1^\infty \mu_{A_{E_l}}(x)\,dx}\right) = \min_{l \in R}\left(\frac{\int_1^l x\,\overline{\mu}_{\hat{A}}(x)\,dx + \int_{l+1}^\infty x\,\underline{\mu}_{\hat{A}}(x)\,dx}{\int_1^l \overline{\mu}_{\hat{A}}(x)\,dx + \int_{l+1}^\infty \underline{\mu}_{\hat{A}}(x)\,dx}\right) \tag{20}$$

$$c_r(\hat{D}) = max \text{ \{centroid of all embedded T1 FSs in DOU}(\hat{D})\} = max_{r \in R}\left(C(A_{E_r})\right)$$

$$c_r(\hat{D}) = \max_{r \in R}\left(\frac{\int_1^\infty x\,\mu_{A_{E_r}}(x)\,dx}{\int_1^\infty \mu_{A_{E_r}}(x)\,dx}\right) = \max_{r \in R}\left(\frac{\int_1^r x\,\underline{\mu}_{\hat{A}}(x)\,dx + \int_{r+1}^\infty x\,\overline{\mu}_{\hat{A}}(x)\,dx}{\int_1^r \underline{\mu}_{\hat{A}}(x)\,dx + \int_{r+1}^\infty \overline{\mu}_{\hat{A}}(x)\,dx}\right), \tag{21}$$

in which $\mu_{A_{E_l}}$ and $\mu_{A_{E_r}}$ denote embedded type-1 fuzzy sets as the following:

$$\mu_{A_{E_l}}(x) = \begin{cases} \overline{\mu}_{\hat{A}}(x), & if\ x \le l, \\ \underline{\mu}_{\hat{A}}(x), & if\ x > l, \end{cases} \tag{22}$$

$$\mu_{A_{E_l}}(x) = \begin{cases} \underline{\mu}_{\hat{A}}(x), & if\ x \le r, \\ \overline{\mu}_{\hat{A}}(x), & if\ x > r. \end{cases} \tag{23}$$

where $l, r (\in X_c \subseteq R)$ are switch points that mark the change from $\overline{\mu}_{\hat{A}}(x)$ to $\underline{\mu}_{\hat{A}}(x)$ and from $\underline{\mu}_{\hat{A}}(x)$ to $\overline{\mu}_{\hat{A}}(x)$, respectively. $\underline{\mu}_{\hat{A}}(x)$ and $\overline{\mu}_{\hat{A}}(x)$ are respectively the lower and upper membership functions of $\hat{A}$. See Fig. 5.

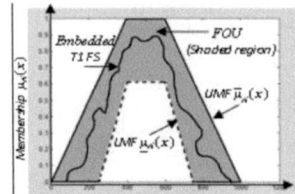 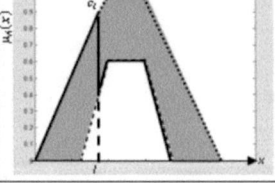 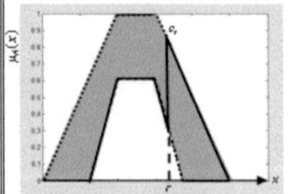

Fig. 5. (a) Interval Type-2 fuzzy set   (b) Explanation of the switch point l   (c) Explanation of the switch

5.1. Derivation of Type-Reduction for Interval T2 FLS

The general form for continuous domain in order to calculate the different kinds of type-reduced can all be given by, [12-13], [17], [20]:

$$Y_{TR}(\mathbb{Y}^1, \dots, \mathbb{Y}^\infty, \mathbb{A}^1, \dots, \mathbb{A}^\infty) = \int_{y^1 \in [y_l^1, y_r^1]} \dots \int_{y^\infty \in [y_l^\infty, y_r^\infty]} \int_{a^1 \in [\underline{a}^1, \overline{a}^1]} \dots \int_{a^\infty \in [\underline{a}^\infty, \overline{a}^\infty]} 1 / \frac{\sum_{i=1}^{L=\infty} y^i\,a^i}{\sum_{i=1}^{L=\infty} a^i}, \tag{24}$$

where each one of $y_l^i, y_r^i, \underline{a}^i\ \overline{a}^i\ (i = 1, \dots, \infty)$ and L have various meaning, as follows, [15]:

1. In case of centroid and center of sums be $y_l^i = y_r^i$, the ith point in the sampled universe of discourse of the FLS's output, $\underline{a}^i, \overline{a}^i$ be the single (or sums of all rules for COS) of lower and upper membership degrees for the ith sampled point; contains antecedent and consequent MF parameters, and L is a number of sampled points.

IOSR Journal of Computer Engineering (IOSR-JCE)
e-ISSN: 2278-0661,p-ISSN: 2278-8727,
PP 45-57
www.iosrjournals.org

2. In case of centre of sets be y_l^i, y_r^i left and right endpoints of the centroid of the consequent of ith rule. While with height TR is $y_l^i = y_r^i$, a single point in the consequent domain of ith rules, treated as a consequent parameter. In the COS and height TR, $\underline{a}^i, \overline{a}^i$ be lower and upper firing degrees for the ith rule; contains antecedent MF parameters, and L is a number of rules.

Because all the memberships in an interval type-1 set are crisp then we represent an interval set by its domain interval. It can be represented by its canter and spread as $[c - s, c + s]$, where $c = (r + l)/2$ and $s = (r - l)/2$, where l left and r right endpoints. Each $\mathbb{Y}^i$ in (24) is an IT1 S having centre $c_\mathbb{Y}^i$ and spread $s_\mathbb{Y}^i \geq 0$. Each $\mathbb{A}^i$ is also IT1 S with centre $c_\mathbb{A}^i$ and spread $s_\mathbb{A}^i \geq 0$ (suppose $c_\mathbb{A}^i \geq s_\mathbb{A}^i, \forall\, i = 1, \dots, \infty$). Therefore, we need to calculate its two endpoints $[y_l, y_r]$.

Now, we assume that,

$$S(a^i, \dots, a^{L=\infty}) = \frac{\int_{i=1}^{L=\infty} y^i\, a^i}{\int_{i=1}^{L=\infty} a^i} \tag{25}$$

where $a^i \in \left[c_\mathbb{A}^i - s_\mathbb{A}^i, c_\mathbb{A}^i + s_\mathbb{A}^i\right]$ and $y^i \in \left[c_\mathbb{Y}^i - s_\mathbb{Y}^i, c_\mathbb{Y}^i + s_\mathbb{Y}^i\right]$. Next, we explain an iterative procedure to compute left end-point, $y_l = \min(S)$, and right endpoint, $y_r = \max(S)$, for IT2 FLS.

In order to compute $(\min(S))$, we put $y^i = c_\mathbb{Y}^i - s_\mathbb{Y}^i$ $(i = 1, \dots, \infty)$ and suppose $y^1 \leq y^2 \leq \dots \leq y^\infty$, then,

a) Put $a^i = c_\mathbb{A}^i$, $i = 1, \dots, \infty$ and calculated $S' = S(c_\mathbb{A}^1, \dots, c_\mathbb{A}^\infty)$ by using (25);

b) Find $1 \leq h \leq \infty$ s.t. $y^h \leq S' \leq y^{h+e}$, where e is a so small real number;

c) We put $a^i = c_\mathbb{A}^i + s_\mathbb{A}^i$, $\forall\, i \in [1, h]$ and $a^i = c_\mathbb{A}^i - s_\mathbb{A}^i$, $\forall\, i \in [h + e, \infty)$, thus compute S'' using (25) as follows:

$$S'' = S\left((c_\mathbb{A}^1 + s_\mathbb{A}^1), \dots, (c_\mathbb{A}^h + s_\mathbb{A}^h), (c_\mathbb{A}^{h+e} - s_\mathbb{A}^{h+e}), \dots, (c_\mathbb{A}^\infty - s_\mathbb{A}^\infty)\right) \tag{26}$$

d) If $S'' = S'$, then stop and put S'' is the minimum value of S; else continue.

e) Put $S' = S''$ go back to step b.

For compute $(\max(S))$, we put $y^i = c_\mathbb{Y}^i + s_\mathbb{Y}^i$ $(i = 1, \dots, \infty)$, and suppose $y^1 \leq y^2 \leq \dots \leq y^\infty$. Therefore

a) Put $a^i = c_\mathbb{A}^i$, $i = 1, \dots, \infty$ and calculate $S' = S(c_\mathbb{A}^1, \dots, c_\mathbb{A}^\infty)$ by using (25);

b) Find h $(1 \leq h \leq \infty)$ s.t. $y^h \leq S' \leq y^{h+e}$, where e is a very small real number;

c) We put $a^i = c_\mathbb{A}^i - s_\mathbb{A}^i$, $\forall\, i \in [1, h]$ and $a^i = c_\mathbb{A}^i + s_\mathbb{A}^i$, $\forall\, i \in [h + e, \infty)$, thus compute S'' using (25) as follows:

$$S'' = S\left((c_\mathbb{A}^1 - s_\mathbb{A}^1), \dots, (c_\mathbb{A}^h - s_\mathbb{A}^h), (c_\mathbb{A}^{h+e} + s_\mathbb{A}^{h+e}), \dots, (c_\mathbb{A}^\infty + s_\mathbb{A}^\infty)\right) \tag{27}$$

d) If $S'' = S'$, then stop and put S'' is the maximum value of S; else continue;

e) Put $S' = S''$ go back to step b.

This procedure of computational can be used to calculate the TR set for all of the kind reducers, with a great reduction in computational complexity.

5.2. Defuzzification

Since Y_{TR} is an interval set for all kinds of type-reduction method, we defuzzify it using the average of y_l and y_r, [11], [13], [18], therefore, the defuzzified output of IT2 FLS is

$$y(\mathrm{x}) = \frac{c_l + c_r}{2} \tag{28}$$

6. APPLICATION OF AN IT2 FLS

The purpose of this section is to provide real medical application for the IT2 *FLS*. The mathematical operations in an IT2 *FLS* are explained using an application. This application cares about the heart diseases, where we are able to determine the status of the heart for the people who suffer from heart disease or not, that depend a range of analyzes and tests performed for each person. Application of the heart disease contains thirteen attributes (which have been extracted from a larger set of 75): Age; Sex; Chest pain type; Resting blood pressure; Serum cholesterol in mg/dl; Fasting blood sugar;

IOSR Journal of Computer Engineering (IOSR-JCE)
e-ISSN: 2278-0661,p-ISSN: 2278-8727,
PP 45-57
www.iosrjournals.org

Resting electrocardiographic results; Maximum heart rate achieved; Exercise induced angina; Old peak (ST depression induced by exercise relative to rest); The slope of the peak exercise ST segment; Number of major vessels that colored by fluoroscopy; and Thal: Normal, fixed defect, and reversible defect. This data was obtained from "StatLib. http://datamarket.com/data/set/22vj/". The prediction variable (output) is an absence or presence of heart disease. There are 270 observations, and no missing values.

6.1. Discussion and Simulation Results

Consider an IT2 FLS that has thirteen inputs $(x_1, x_2, ..., x_{13})$ and one output y. Each input domain consists of maximum four IT2 FSs, which are trapezoids LMFs and UMFs, and theirs FOUs shown in Figure. 6.

The rule-base of the IT2 FLS has multi models for rules as the following:

R^1: if x_1 is $\hat{A}_{1,3} \wedge x_2$ is $\hat{A}_{2,1} \wedge x_3$ is $\hat{A}_{3,3} \wedge x_4$ is $\hat{A}_{4,1} \wedge x_5$ is $\hat{A}_{5,3} \wedge x_6$ is $\hat{A}_{6,1} \wedge x_7$ is $\hat{A}_{7,3} \wedge x_8$ is $\hat{A}_{8,2} \wedge x_9$ is $\hat{A}_{9,1}$
$\wedge x_{10}$ is $\hat{A}_{10,2} \wedge x_{11}$ is $\hat{A}_{11,2} \wedge x_{12}$ is $\hat{A}_{12,1} \wedge x_{13}$ is $\hat{A}_{13,3}$ then y is Y^1

R^2: if x_1 is $\hat{A}_{1,2} \wedge x_2$ is $\hat{A}_{2,1} \wedge x_3$ is $\hat{A}_{3,2} \wedge x_4$ is $\hat{A}_{4,1} \wedge x_5$ is $\hat{A}_{5,1} \wedge x_6$ is $\hat{A}_{6,1} \wedge x_7$ is $\hat{A}_{7,1} \wedge x_8$ is $\hat{A}_{8,3} \wedge x_9$ is $\hat{A}_{9,1}$
$\wedge x_{10}$ is $\hat{A}_{10,1} \wedge x_{11}$ is $\hat{A}_{11,1} \wedge x_{12}$ is $\hat{A}_{12,1} \wedge x_{13}$ is $\hat{A}_{13,1}$ then y is Y^1

$\vdots$

R^n: if x_1 is $\hat{A}_{1,1} \wedge x_2$ is $\hat{A}_{2,2} \wedge x_3$ is $\hat{A}_{3,4} \wedge x_4$ is $\hat{A}_{4,2} \wedge x_5$ is $\hat{A}_{5,1} \wedge x_6$ is $\hat{A}_{6,1} \wedge x_7$ is $\hat{A}_{7,1} \wedge x_8$ is $\hat{A}_{8,2} \wedge x_9$ is $\hat{A}_{9,2}$
$\wedge x_{10}$ is $\hat{A}_{10,2} \wedge x_{11}$ is $\hat{A}_{11,2} \wedge x_{12}$ is $\hat{A}_{12,1} \wedge x_{13}$ is $\hat{A}_{13,3}$ then y is Y^2

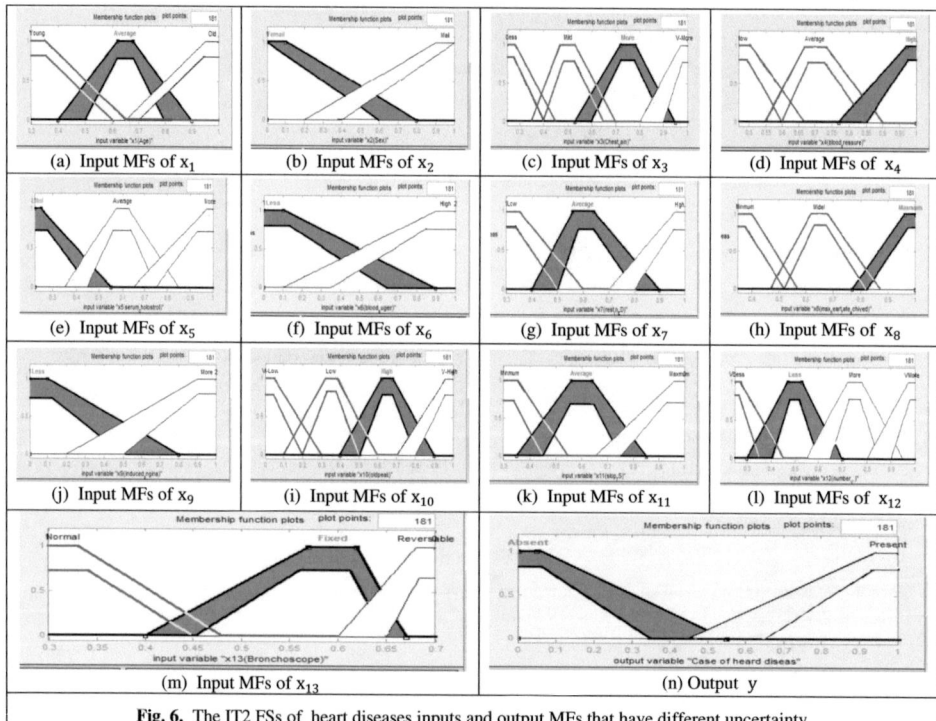

(a) Input MFs of x_1	(b) Input MFs of x_2	(c) Input MFs of x_3	(d) Input MFs of x_4
(e) Input MFs of x_5	(f) Input MFs of x_6	(g) Input MFs of x_7	(h) Input MFs of x_8
(j) Input MFs of x_9	(i) Input MFs of x_{10}	(k) Input MFs of x_{11}	(l) Input MFs of x_{12}
(m) Input MFs of x_{13}		(n) Output y	

Fig. 6. The IT2 FSs of heart diseases inputs and output MFs that have different uncertainty

There are 270 observations of heart diseases divided into two parts: the first part contains 150 cases were the heart disease absence, and the second part contains 120 cases were the heart disease presence. Each case that has thirteen an inputs are described by IT2 FSs. Consider one case of an input vector,

IOSR Journal of Computer Engineering (IOSR-JCE)
e-ISSN: 2278-0661,p-ISSN: 2278-8727,
PP 45-57
www.iosrjournals.org

$x' = (x_1', x_2', x_3', x_4', x_5', x_6', x_7', x_8', x_9', x_{10}', x_{11}', x_{12}', x_{13}') = (0.87, 0.01, 0.78, 0.55, 0.95, 0.14, 0.94, 0.79, 0.14, 0.26, 0.6, 0.27, 0.69)$

The firing intervals for the first fifth rules at an input vector x' are as the following (see Table 1):

For this an input vector x', we must repeat this procedure for all rules. The firing intervals of the rules are computed using the minimum function as the following:

$$R^1: [\underline{a}^1, \bar{a}^1] = \begin{bmatrix} \min\{\mu_{\underline{A}_{1,3}}(x_1'), \mu_{\underline{A}_{2,1}}(x_2'), \mu_{\underline{A}_{3,3}}(x_3'), \mu_{\underline{A}_{4,1}}(x_4'), \mu_{\underline{A}_{5,3}}(x_5'), \mu_{\underline{A}_{6,1}}(x_6'), \mu_{\underline{A}_{7,3}}(x_7'), \mu_{\underline{A}_{8,2}}(x_8'), \mu_{\underline{A}_{9,1}}(x_9'), \mu_{\underline{A}_{10,2}}(x_{10}'), \mu_{\underline{A}_{11,2}}(x_{11}'), \mu_{\underline{A}_{12,1}}(x_{12}'), \mu_{\underline{A}_{13,3}}(x_{13}')\}, \\ \min\{\mu_{\bar{A}_{1,3}}(x_1'), \mu_{\bar{A}_{2,1}}(x_2'), \mu_{\bar{A}_{3,3}}(x_3'), \mu_{\bar{A}_{4,1}}(x_4'), \mu_{\bar{A}_{5,3}}(x_5'), \mu_{\bar{A}_{6,1}}(x_6'), \mu_{\bar{A}_{7,3}}(x_7'), \mu_{\bar{A}_{8,2}}(x_8'), \mu_{\bar{A}_{9,1}}(x_9'), \mu_{\bar{A}_{10,2}}(x_{10}'), \mu_{\bar{A}_{11,2}}(x_{11}'), \mu_{\bar{A}_{12,1}}(x_{12}'), \mu_{\bar{A}_{13,3}}(x_{13}')\} \end{bmatrix}$$

$$R^1: [\underline{a}^1, \bar{a}^1] = \begin{bmatrix} \min\{0.56, 0.8, 0.793, 0.38, 0.7, 0.68, 0.7, 0.18, 0.7, 0.4, 0.7, 0.75, 0.75\}, \\ \min\{0.73, 0.998, 0.994, 0.7, 0.94, 0.95, 0.923, 0.42, 0.94, 0.73, 1, 0.994, 1\} \end{bmatrix} = [0.18, 0.42]$$

$$R^2: [\underline{a}^2, \bar{a}^2] = \begin{bmatrix} \min\{\mu_{\underline{A}_{1,2}}(x_1'), \mu_{\underline{A}_{2,1}}(x_2'), \mu_{\underline{A}_{3,2}}(x_3'), \mu_{\underline{A}_{4,1}}(x_4'), \mu_{\underline{A}_{5,1}}(x_5'), \mu_{\underline{A}_{6,1}}(x_6'), \mu_{\underline{A}_{7,1}}(x_7'), \mu_{\underline{A}_{8,3}}(x_8'), \mu_{\underline{A}_{9,1}}(x_9'), \mu_{\underline{A}_{10,1}}(x_{10}'), \mu_{\underline{A}_{11,1}}(x_{11}'), \mu_{\underline{A}_{12,1}}(x_{12}'), \mu_{\underline{A}_{13,1}}(x_{13}')\}, \\ \min\{\mu_{\bar{A}_{1,2}}(x_1'), \mu_{\bar{A}_{2,1}}(x_2'), \mu_{\bar{A}_{3,2}}(x_3'), \mu_{\bar{A}_{4,1}}(x_4'), \mu_{\bar{A}_{5,1}}(x_5'), \mu_{\bar{A}_{6,1}}(x_6'), \mu_{\bar{A}_{7,1}}(x_7'), \mu_{\bar{A}_{8,3}}(x_8'), \mu_{\bar{A}_{9,1}}(x_9'), \mu_{\bar{A}_{10,1}}(x_{10}'), \mu_{\bar{A}_{11,1}}(x_{11}'), \mu_{\bar{A}_{12,1}}(x_{12}'), \mu_{\bar{A}_{13,1}}(x_{13}')\} \end{bmatrix}$$

$$R^2: [\underline{a}^2, \bar{a}^2] = \begin{bmatrix} \min\{0.6, 0.98, 0.7, 0.54, 0.39, 0.68, 0.65, 0.17, 0.7, 0.75, 0.6, 0.75, 0.67\}, \\ \min\{0.86, 1, 0.999, 0.82, 0.63, 0.95, 0.92, 0.42, 0.94, 1, 0.95, 0.999, 0.87\} \end{bmatrix} = [0.17, 0.42],$$

$\vdots$

$$R^n: [\underline{a}^n, \bar{a}^n] = \begin{bmatrix} \min\{\mu_{\underline{A}_{1,1}}(x_1'), \mu_{\underline{A}_{2,2}}(x_2'), \mu_{\underline{A}_{3,4}}(x_3'), \mu_{\underline{A}_{4,2}}(x_4'), \mu_{\underline{A}_{5,1}}(x_5'), \mu_{\underline{A}_{6,1}}(x_6'), \mu_{\underline{A}_{7,1}}(x_7'), \mu_{\underline{A}_{8,2}}(x_8'), \mu_{\underline{A}_{9,2}}(x_9'), \mu_{\underline{A}_{10,2}}(x_{10}'), \mu_{\underline{A}_{11,2}}(x_{11}'), \mu_{\underline{A}_{12,1}}(x_{12}'), \mu_{\underline{A}_{13,3}}(x_{13}')\}, \\ \min\{\mu_{\bar{A}_{1,1}}(x_1'), \mu_{\bar{A}_{2,2}}(x_2'), \mu_{\bar{A}_{3,4}}(x_3'), \mu_{\bar{A}_{4,2}}(x_4'), \mu_{\bar{A}_{5,1}}(x_5'), \mu_{\bar{A}_{6,1}}(x_6'), \mu_{\bar{A}_{7,1}}(x_7'), \mu_{\bar{A}_{8,2}}(x_8'), \mu_{\bar{A}_{9,2}}(x_9'), \mu_{\bar{A}_{10,2}}(x_{10}'), \mu_{\bar{A}_{11,2}}(x_{11}'), \mu_{\bar{A}_{12,1}}(x_{12}'), \mu_{\bar{A}_{13,3}}(x_{13}')\} \end{bmatrix}$$

$$R^n: [\underline{a}^n, \bar{a}^n] = \begin{bmatrix} \min\{0.5, 0.83, 0.75, 0.2, 0.43, 0.68, 0.65, 0.8, 0.7, 033, 0.7, 0.75, 0.75\}, \\ \min\{0.67, 1, 0.999, 0.58, 0.67, 0.95, 0.92, 1, 0.97, 0.68, 1, 0.999, 1\} \end{bmatrix} = [0.2, 0.58]$$

Table 1. The firing intervals for the rules at an input vector x'

No	R^1	R^2	R^3	R^4	R^5	R^6	..	R^n
x_1	$[\mu_{\underline{A}_{1,3}}(x_1'),\mu_{\bar{A}_{1,3}}(x_1')] = [0.56,0.73]$	$[\mu_{\underline{A}_{1,2}}(x_1'),\mu_{\bar{A}_{1,2}}(x_1')] = [0.6,0.86]$	$[\mu_{\underline{A}_{1,2}}(x_1'),\mu_{\bar{A}_{1,2}}(x_1')] = [0.8,1]$	$[\mu_{\underline{A}_{1,2}}(x_1'),\mu_{\bar{A}_{1,2}}(x_1')] = [0.8,1]$	$[\mu_{\underline{A}_{1,3}}(x_1'),\mu_{\bar{A}_{1,3}}(x_1')] = [0.13,0.55]$	$[\mu_{\underline{A}_{1,2}}(x_1'),\mu_{\bar{A}_{1,2}}(x_1')] = [0.47,0.63]$	..	$[\mu_{\underline{A}_{1,1}}(x_1'),\mu_{\bar{A}_{1,1}}(x_1')] = [0.5,0.67]$
x_2	$[\mu_{\underline{A}_{2,1}}(x_2'),\mu_{\bar{A}_{2,1}}(x_2')] = [0.8,0.998]$	$[\mu_{\underline{A}_{2,1}}(x_2'),\mu_{\bar{A}_{2,1}}(x_2')] = [0.98,1]$	$[\mu_{\underline{A}_{2,2}}(x_2'),\mu_{\bar{A}_{2,2}}(x_2')] = [0.83,1]$	$[\mu_{\underline{A}_{2,2}}(x_2'),\mu_{\bar{A}_{2,2}}(x_2')] = [0.83,1]$	$[\mu_{\underline{A}_{2,2}}(x_2'),\mu_{\bar{A}_{2,2}}(x_2')] = [0.98,1]$	$[\mu_{\underline{A}_{2,2}}(x_2'),\mu_{\bar{A}_{2,2}}(x_2')] = [0.83,1]$	..	$[\mu_{\underline{A}_{2,2}}(x_2'),\mu_{\bar{A}_{2,2}}(x_2')] = [0.83,1]$
x_3	$[\mu_{\underline{A}_{3,3}}(x_3'),\mu_{\bar{A}_{3,3}}(x_3')] = [0.793,0.994]$	$[\mu_{\underline{A}_{3,2}}(x_3'),\mu_{\bar{A}_{3,2}}(x_3')] = [0.7,0.999]$	$[\mu_{\underline{A}_{3,4}}(x_3'),\mu_{\bar{A}_{3,4}}(x_3')] = [0.75,0.999]$	$[\mu_{\underline{A}_{3,4}}(x_3'),\mu_{\bar{A}_{3,4}}(x_3')] = [0.75,0.99]$	$[\mu_{\underline{A}_{3,1}}(x_3'),\mu_{\bar{A}_{3,1}}(x_3')] = [0.75,0.99]$	$[\mu_{\underline{A}_{3,4}}(x_3'),\mu_{\bar{A}_{3,4}}(x_3')] = [0.8,1]$	..	$[\mu_{\underline{A}_{3,4}}(x_3'),\mu_{\bar{A}_{3,4}}(x_3')] = [0.75,0.99]$
x_4	$[\mu_{\underline{A}_{4,1}}(x_4'),\mu_{\bar{A}_{4,1}}(x_4')] = [0.38,0.7]$	$[\mu_{\underline{A}_{4,1}}(x_4'),\mu_{\bar{A}_{4,1}}(x_4')] = [0.54,0.82]$	$[\mu_{\underline{A}_{4,2}}(x_4'),\mu_{\bar{A}_{4,2}}(x_4')] = [0.8,1]$	$[\mu_{\underline{A}_{4,1}}(x_4'),\mu_{\bar{A}_{4,1}}(x_4')] = [0.46,0.76]$	$[\mu_{\underline{A}_{4,2}}(x_4'),\mu_{\bar{A}_{4,2}}(x_4')] = [0.67,0.88]$	$[\mu_{\underline{A}_{4,2}}(x_4'),\mu_{\bar{A}_{4,2}}(x_4')] = [0.8,1]$	..	$[\mu_{\underline{A}_{4,2}}(x_4'),\mu_{\bar{A}_{4,2}}(x_4')] = [0.2,0.58]$
x_5	$[\mu_{\underline{A}_{5,3}}(x_5'),\mu_{\bar{A}_{5,3}}(x_5')] = [0.7,0.94]$	$[\mu_{\underline{A}_{5,1}}(x_5'),\mu_{\bar{A}_{5,1}}(x_5')] = [0.39,0.63]$	$[\mu_{\underline{A}_{5,2}}(x_5'),\mu_{\bar{A}_{5,2}}(x_5')] = [0.067,0.5]$	$[\mu_{\underline{A}_{5,2}}(x_5'),\mu_{\bar{A}_{5,2}}(x_5')] = [0.7,1]$	$[\mu_{\underline{A}_{5,2}}(x_5'),\mu_{\bar{A}_{5,2}}(x_5')] = [0.067,0.5]$	$[\mu_{\underline{A}_{5,1}}(x_5'),\mu_{\bar{A}_{5,1}}(x_5')] = [0.33,0.68]$	..	$[\mu_{\underline{A}_{5,1}}(x_5'),\mu_{\bar{A}_{5,1}}(x_5')] = [0.43,0.67]$
x_6	$[\mu_{\underline{A}_{6,1}}(x_6'),\mu_{\bar{A}_{6,1}}(x_6')] = [0.68,0.95]$	$[\mu_{\underline{A}_{6,1}}(x_6'),\mu_{\bar{A}_{6,1}}(x_6')] = [0.68,0.95]$	$[\mu_{\underline{A}_{6,1}}(x_6'),\mu_{\bar{A}_{6,1}}(x_6')] = [0.68,0.95]$	$[\mu_{\underline{A}_{6,2}}(x_6'),\mu_{\bar{A}_{6,2}}(x_6')] = [0.8,1]$	$[\mu_{\underline{A}_{6,2}}(x_6'),\mu_{\bar{A}_{6,2}}(x_6')] = [0.68,0.95]$	$[\mu_{\underline{A}_{6,1}}(x_6'),\mu_{\bar{A}_{6,1}}(x_6')] = [0.8,1]$	..	$[\mu_{\underline{A}_{6,1}}(x_6'),\mu_{\bar{A}_{6,1}}(x_6')] = [0.68,0.95]$
x_7	$[\mu_{\underline{A}_{7,3}}(x_7'),\mu_{\bar{A}_{7,3}}(x_7')] = [0.7,0.923]$	$[\mu_{\underline{A}_{7,1}}(x_7'),\mu_{\bar{A}_{7,1}}(x_7')] = [0.65,0.92]$	$[\mu_{\underline{A}_{7,3}}(x_7'),\mu_{\bar{A}_{7,3}}(x_7')] = [0.7,0.923]$	$[\mu_{\underline{A}_{7,1}}(x_7'),\mu_{\bar{A}_{7,1}}(x_7')] = [0.65,0.92]$	$[\mu_{\underline{A}_{7,3}}(x_7'),\mu_{\bar{A}_{7,3}}(x_7')] = [0.7,0.921]$	$[\mu_{\underline{A}_{7,3}}(x_7'),\mu_{\bar{A}_{7,3}}(x_7')] = [0.7,0.92]$	..	$[\mu_{\underline{A}_{7,1}}(x_7'),\mu_{\bar{A}_{7,1}}(x_7')] = [0.65,0.92]$
x_8	$[\mu_{\underline{A}_{8,2}}(x_8'),\mu_{\bar{A}_{8,2}}(x_8')] = [0.18,0.42]$	$[\mu_{\underline{A}_{8,3}}(x_8'),\mu_{\bar{A}_{8,3}}(x_8')] = [0.17,0.42]$	$[\mu_{\underline{A}_{8,3}}(x_8'),\mu_{\bar{A}_{8,3}}(x_8')] = [0.55,0.79]$	$[\mu_{\underline{A}_{8,2}}(x_8'),\mu_{\bar{A}_{8,2}}(x_8')] = [0.53,0.74]$	$[\mu_{\underline{A}_{8,3}}(x_8'),\mu_{\bar{A}_{8,3}}(x_8')] = [0.29,0.53]$	$[\mu_{\underline{A}_{8,2}}(x_8'),\mu_{\bar{A}_{8,2}}(x_8')] = [0.22,0.47]$	..	$[\mu_{\underline{A}_{8,2}}(x_8'),\mu_{\bar{A}_{8,2}}(x_8')] = [0.8,1]$
x_9	$[\mu_{\underline{A}_{9,1}}(x_9'),\mu_{\bar{A}_{9,1}}(x_9')] = [0.7,0.94]$	$[\mu_{\underline{A}_{9,1}}(x_9'),\mu_{\bar{A}_{9,1}}(x_9')] = [0.7,0.94]$	$[\mu_{\underline{A}_{9,2}}(x_9'),\mu_{\bar{A}_{9,2}}(x_9')] = [0.7,0.97]$	$[\mu_{\underline{A}_{9,1}}(x_9'),\mu_{\bar{A}_{9,1}}(x_9')] = [0.7,0.94]$	$[\mu_{\underline{A}_{9,1}}(x_9'),\mu_{\bar{A}_{9,1}}(x_9')] = [0.7,0.94]$	$[\mu_{\underline{A}_{9,2}}(x_9'),\mu_{\bar{A}_{9,2}}(x_9')] = [0.7,0.94]$	..	$[\mu_{\underline{A}_{9,2}}(x_9'),\mu_{\bar{A}_{9,2}}(x_9')] = [0.7,0.97]$
x_{10}	$[\mu_{\underline{A}_{10,2}}(x_{10}'),\mu_{\bar{A}_{10,2}}(x_{10}')] = [0.4,0.73]$	$[\mu_{\underline{A}_{10,1}}(x_{10}'),\mu_{\bar{A}_{10,1}}(x_{10}')] = [0.75,1]$	$[\mu_{\underline{A}_{10,1}}(x_{10}'),\mu_{\bar{A}_{10,1}}(x_{10}')] = [0.75,1]$	$[\mu_{\underline{A}_{10,1}}(x_{10}'),\mu_{\bar{A}_{10,1}}(x_{10}')] = [0.75,1]$	$[\mu_{\underline{A}_{10,2}}(x_{10}'),\mu_{\bar{A}_{10,2}}(x_{10}')] = [0.53,0.82]$	$[\mu_{\underline{A}_{10,2}}(x_{10}'),\mu_{\bar{A}_{10,2}}(x_{10}')] = [40.2,0.59]$	..	$[\mu_{\underline{A}_{10,2}}(x_{10}'),\mu_{\bar{A}_{10,2}}(x_{10}')] = [0.33,0.68]$
x_{11}	$[\mu_{\underline{A}_{11,2}}(x_{11}'),\mu_{\bar{A}_{11,2}}(x_{11}')] = [0.7,1]$	$[\mu_{\underline{A}_{11,1}}(x_{11}'),\mu_{\bar{A}_{11,1}}(x_{11}')] = [0.6,0.95]$	$[\mu_{\underline{A}_{11,1}}(x_{11}'),\mu_{\bar{A}_{11,1}}(x_{11}')] = [0.6,0.95]$	$[\mu_{\underline{A}_{11,1}}(x_{11}'),\mu_{\bar{A}_{11,1}}(x_{11}')] = [0.6,0.95]$	$[\mu_{\underline{A}_{11,2}}(x_{11}'),\mu_{\bar{A}_{11,2}}(x_{11}')] = [0.7,1]$	$[\mu_{\underline{A}_{11,2}}(x_{11}'),\mu_{\bar{A}_{11,2}}(x_{11}')] = [0.7,1]$	..	$[\mu_{\underline{A}_{11,2}}(x_{11}'),\mu_{\bar{A}_{11,2}}(x_{11}')] = [0.7,1]$
x_{12}	$[\mu_{\underline{A}_{12,1}}(x_{12}'),\mu_{\bar{A}_{12,1}}(x_{12}')] = [0.75,0.994]$	$[\mu_{\underline{A}_{12,1}}(x_{12}'),\mu_{\bar{A}_{12,1}}(x_{12}')] = [0.75,0.994]$	$[\mu_{\underline{A}_{12,1}}(x_{12}'),\mu_{\bar{A}_{12,1}}(x_{12}')] = [0.75,0.994]$	$[\mu_{\underline{A}_{12,4}}(x_{12}'),\mu_{\bar{A}_{12,4}}(x_{12}')] = [0.5,0.88]$	$[\mu_{\underline{A}_{12,1}}(x_{12}'),\mu_{\bar{A}_{12,1}}(x_{12}')] = [0.75,1]$	$[\mu_{\underline{A}_{12,3}}(x_{12}'),\mu_{\bar{A}_{12,3}}(x_{12}')] = [0.75,0.999]$	..	$[\mu_{\underline{A}_{12,1}}(x_{12}'),\mu_{\bar{A}_{12,1}}(x_{12}')] = [0.75,0.999]$
x_{13}	$[\mu_{\underline{A}_{13,3}}(x_{13}'),\mu_{\bar{A}_{13,3}}(x_{13}')] = [0.75,1]$	$[\mu_{\underline{A}_{13,1}}(x_{13}'),\mu_{\bar{A}_{13,1}}(x_{13}')] = [0.67,0.87]$	$[\mu_{\underline{A}_{13,2}}(x_{13}'),\mu_{\bar{A}_{13,2}}(x_{13}')] = [0.6,0.8]$	$[\mu_{\underline{A}_{13,3}}(x_{13}'),\mu_{\bar{A}_{13,3}}(x_{13}')] = [0.75,1]$	$[\mu_{\underline{A}_{13,2}}(x_{13}'),\mu_{\bar{A}_{13,2}}(x_{13}')] = [0.75,0.994]$	$[\mu_{\underline{A}_{13,3}}(x_{13}'),\mu_{\bar{A}_{13,3}}(x_{13}')] = [0.7,0.999]$	..	$[\mu_{\underline{A}_{13,3}}(x_{13}'),\mu_{\bar{A}_{13,3}}(x_{13}')] = [0.75,1]$

We have to complete these procedures for all rules. Consequently, we obtain the Table 2.

The TR for an IT2 FLS uses the *iterative* KM algorithms, this may cause a computational bottleneck, even for real medical applications of the IT2 FLSs, where it has been demonstrated that very good performance can be satisfied by doing this. From (20) and (21), we are calculated left and right endpoints $[y_l, y_r]$ as follows:

IOSR Journal of Computer Engineering (IOSR-JCE)
e-ISSN: 2278-0661,p-ISSN: 2278-8727,
PP 45-57
www.iosrjournals.org

$$y_l = \frac{\underline{a}^1 \underline{y}^1 + \underline{a}^2 \underline{y}^2 + \underline{a}^3 \underline{y}^3 + \underline{a}^4 \underline{y}^4 + \underline{a}^5 \underline{y}^5 + \underline{a}^6 \underline{y}^6 + \cdots + \underline{a}^n \underline{y}^n}{\underline{a}^1 + \underline{a}^2 + \underline{a}^3 + \underline{a}^4 + \underline{a}^5 + \underline{a}^6 + \cdots + \underline{a}^n},$$

$$y_l = \frac{0.42(0.146) + 0.17(0.149) + 0.067(0.18) + 0.46(0.162) + 0.067(0.91) + 0.2(0.896) + \cdots + 0.2(0.949)}{0.42 + 0.17 + 0.067 + 0.46 + 0.067 + 0.2 + \cdots + 0.2},$$

$$y_r = \frac{\underline{a}^1 \overline{y}^1 + \underline{a}^2 \overline{y}^2 + \underline{a}^3 \overline{y}^3 + \underline{a}^4 \overline{y}^4 + \underline{a}^5 \overline{y}^5 + \underline{a}^6 \overline{y}^6 + \cdots + \overline{a}^n \overline{y}^n}{\underline{a}^1 + \underline{a}^2 + \underline{a}^3 + \underline{a}^4 + \underline{a}^5 + \underline{a}^6 + \cdots + \overline{a}^n},$$

$$y_r = \frac{0.18(0.228) + 0.17(0.23) + 0.067(0.19) + 0.46(0.174) + 0.067(0.92) + 0.2(0.96) + \cdots + 0.58(0.96)}{0.18 + 0.17 + 0.067 + 0.46 + 0.067 + 0.2 + \cdots + 0.58}.$$

Therefore, we obtained the values of left and right endpoints y_l and y_r, respectively. Finally, we are defuzzified the interval set (output of the IT2 FLS) in order to compute the crisp output y of the IT2 FLS using (28). We repeated all these procedure with each an input vectors (all observations) to compute the crisp output y_i ($i = 1, \dots, 270$) of the IT2 FLS for all cases.

Table 2. The firing intervals and theirs consequents for rules		
No. of rule	Firing Interval	Consequent
R^1	$[\underline{a}^1, \overline{a}^1] = [0.18, 0.42]$	$[\underline{y}^1, \overline{y}^1] = [0.146, 0.228]$
R^2	$[\underline{a}^2, \overline{a}^2] = [0.17, 0.42]$	$[\underline{y}^2, \overline{y}^2] = [0.149, 0.23]$
R^3	$[\underline{a}^3, \overline{a}^3] = [0.067, 0.5]$	$[\underline{y}^3, \overline{y}^3] = [0.18, 0.19]$
R^4	$[\underline{a}^4, \overline{a}^4] = [0.46, 0.74]$	$[\underline{y}^4, \overline{y}^4] = [0.162, 0.174]$
R^5	$[\underline{a}^5, \overline{a}^5] = [0.067, 0.5]$	$[\underline{y}^5, \overline{y}^5] = [0.91, 0.92]$
R^6	$[\underline{a}^6, \overline{a}^6] = [0.2, 0.47]$	$[\underline{y}^6, \overline{y}^6] = [0.896, 0.96]$
:	:	:
R^n	$[\underline{a}^n, \overline{a}^n] = [0.2, 0.58]$	$[\underline{y}^n, \overline{y}^n] = [0.949, 0.96]$

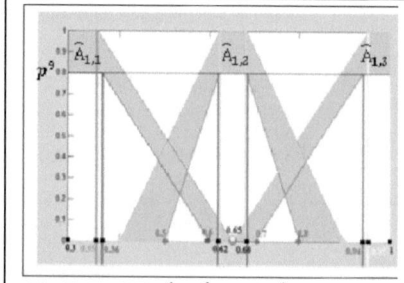

Fig. 7. The MFs $\hat{A}_{1,1}, \hat{A}_{1,2},$ and $\hat{A}_{1,3}$ of the IT2 FLS for the first input

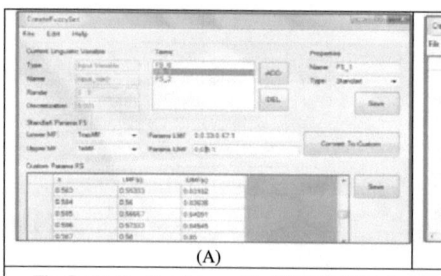

(A)

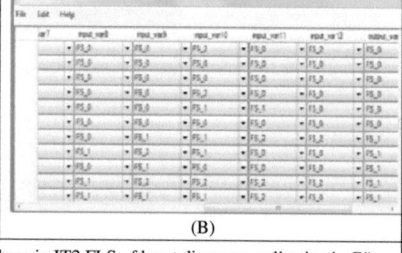

(B)

Fig. 8. (A) Creation fuzzy set in IT2 FLS. (B) Rule-base in IT2 FLS of heart diseases application in C#

Table 3. The various RMSEs of four predicting methods	
Method of model	RMSE
IT2 FLS in MATLAB	0.00075
IT2FLS in visual C#	0.0253
T1 FIS (Mamdani)	0.2441
T1 FIS (Takagi-Sugeno)	0.1988

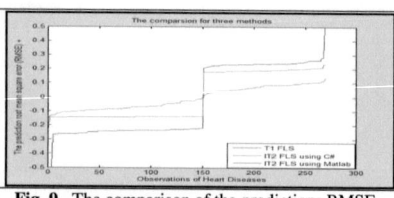

Fig. 9. The comparison of the predictions RMSE for three methods

IOSR Journal of Computer Engineering (IOSR-JCE)
e-ISSN: 2278-0661,p-ISSN: 2278-8727,
PP 45-57
www.iosrjournals.org

6.2. Software Performance

First part the performance of Matlab is used a function "*IT2FLS*" that is provided for computing the output of an IT2 FLS. For performance, the program of "*IT2FLS*" we need to given the rule-base and inputs for the problem. The application is performed using the function "*IT2FLS*". A nine-point vector $[p^1, p^2, \dots, p^9]$ represents each IT2 FS. Therefore, the IT2 FS $\hat{A}_{1,1}$ is represented as (0.3 0.3 0.35 0.65 0.3 0.3 0.36 0.6 0.8), $\hat{A}_{1,2}$ is represented as (0.4 0.62 0.68 0.9 0.5 0.62 0.68 0.8 0.8), and $\hat{A}_{1,3}$ is represented as (0.65 0.95 1 1 0.7 0.94 1 1 0.8), such shown in Figure. 7. Second part of performance is performed using IT2FLS software in visual C# that includes some modules as the linguistic variable, the mf, the rule-base, and the simulator editors. The linguistic variable is used to define the input and the output linguistic variables. The MF is used to define the membership functions related with the linguistic variable. IT2FLS software also allows user to creating and editing rules. The simulator is used to present an interactive view of the logic inference. IT2FLS software does not limit the number of linguistic variables, membership functions of linguistic variables and rules. For our application, we have created the MFs and the rules that are depicted in Figure 8.

6.3. Experimental Comparison

In this subsection, we compare the performance of the four methods. We present results of a comparison of *Heart Diseases (HDs)* using an intelligent architecture between interval type-2 fuzzy logic systems using the IT2FLS in MAT-LAB and the IT2FLS in Visual C# models with type-1 fuzzy inference systems (Mamdani, and Takagi-Sugeno). The prediction root mean square error (RMSE) was 0.00075. Table 3 shows the various RMSE of four predicting methods, where the IT2 FLS in MATLAB and the IT2FLS in Visual C# evaluate the best *HDs* predicts respectively. The advantage of using the IT2FLS predicting method is that it obtains better results, even when data contains high uncertainty. The IT2 provide rather modest performance improvements over the T1 predictor. The comparison of the predictions RMSE for three methods is shown in Fig. 9. Observe from Fig. 9 that: the blue line represents the prediction errors between the actual output of HDs and prediction output using T1 FLS, that has limitation between -0.5 and 0.5; The green line represents the prediction errors using IT2 FLS in C# limited by [-0.1435,0.2325]. While, the prediction errors using IT2 FLS by Matlab has limited by [-0.2194, 0.1385], that are represented by the red line. Note that, the best prediction RMSE when used IT2 FLS by Matlab that was closer to zero.

7. CONCLUSIONS

This work shows that expression (2), which was given by Mendel et al. but on discrete domain, in order to prove an IT2 FS $\hat{A}$ is the union of countable-infinity number of embedded IT2 FSs for a continuous IT2. We extended the derivation of the *union* of *two* IT2 FSs, which was given by Mendel and Bob John, to the *intersection* and *union* of N IT2 FSs, depend on the various concepts such as Theorem 3.1 and 3.2. We presented the *meet* operation of N IT2 FSs depending on the concept of the secondary MF such as Theorem 3.3, which was given by Karnik and Mendel but for the *join* operation. Theorem 4.1 and 4.2 provided the derivation of the relationship between the consequent and the DOU of the T2 fired output for SF and NSF. We have provided the derivation of the general form for continuous domain to calculate the different kinds of type-reduced, which was given by Karnik et al. but for discrete domain. Additionally, we applied the medical application of IT2 FLS's to HDs, in which it demonstrated the basic ideas and the mathematical operations of IT2 fuzzy sets and systems. Finally, we have compared the performance of the four methods of HDs between IT2 FLS using the IT2FLS in MATLAB and the IT2FLS in Visual C# models with T1 FISs (Mamdani, and Takagi-Sugeno). The best result of RMSE was 0.00075 with the IT2FLS in MATLAB. The prediction errors using IT2 FLS in Matlab has limited by [-0.2194, 0.1385], that are represented by the red line that was closer to zero. Our future work includes optimizing the knowledge base of the IT2 FLS, and modelling the IT2 FLS to neural network model on continuous domain.

8. APPENDIX A: THE BASIC CONCEPTS OF TYPE-2 FUZZY SETS

Definition 1: A type-2 fuzzy set, expresses the non-deterministic truth degree with uncertainty for an element that belongs to a set. A type-2 fuzzy set denoted by $\hat{A}$ is described by a *type-2 MF* $\mu_{\hat{A}}(x, u)$, where $x \in X$ and $u \in J_x^u \subseteq [0,1]$, and $0 \le \mu_{\hat{A}}(x, u) \le 1$ is defined as the following:

$$\hat{A} = \{((x, u), \mu_{\hat{A}}(x, u)) \mid \forall x \in X, \forall \ u \in J_x^u \subseteq [0,1]\} \qquad (1.A)$$

It can also be expressed as:

$$\hat{A} = \int_{x \in X} \int_{u \in J_x^u} \mu_{\hat{A}}(x, u)/(x, u), \quad J_x^u \subseteq [0,1], \qquad (2.A)$$

IOSR Journal of Computer Engineering (IOSR-JCE)
e-ISSN: 2278-0661,p-ISSN: 2278-8727,
PP 45-57
www.iosrjournals.org

where $\iint$ denotes union over all allowable x and u. When uncertainties disappear, a T2 MF must reduce to a T1 MF, in which the variable u equals $\mu_{\tilde{A}}(x,u)$, and the third dimension disappears. The amplitudes of a MF should locate between or be equal to zero and one. If all $\mu_{\tilde{A}}(x,u)$ equal to one then $\hat{A}$ is an *interval T2 FS* (IT2 FS).

Definition 2: At each value of x, say $x = a$, the 2-dimentional plane whose axes are u and $\mu_{\tilde{A}}(a,u)$ is called a vertical-slice of $\mu_{\tilde{A}}(x,u)$. A secondary MF is a vertical-slice of $\mu_{\tilde{A}}(x,u)$. It is $\mu_{\tilde{A}}(x = a, u)$ for $a \in X$ and $\forall u \in J_x^u \subseteq [0,1]$, i.e,

$$\mu_{\tilde{A}}(x = a, u) \equiv \mu_{\tilde{A}}(a) = \int_{u \in J_x^u} 1/u, J_x^u \subseteq [0,1]. \tag{3.A}$$

Because $\forall a \in X$, we drop the prime notation on $\mu_{\tilde{A}}(a)$, and refer to $\mu_{\tilde{A}}(x)$ as a secondary MF, the IT2 FS can be expressed (2.A) as the following [10], [12-13], [17]:

$$\hat{A} = \int_{x \in X} \mu_{\tilde{A}}(x)/x = \int_{x \in X} \left[\int_{u \in J_x^u} 1/u \right]/x \tag{4.A}$$

The domain of a secondary MF (J_x^u) is called the primary membership of x, where $J_x^u \subseteq [0,1]$ for $\forall a \in X$.

Definition 3: The *amplitude* of a secondary MF is called a *secondary degree*. The secondary degrees of an IT2 FS are all equal to one. If x and J_x^u are both continuous, then the right-hand side of (4.A) can be denoted as:

$$\hat{A} = \int_{x \in X} \left[\int_{u \in J_x^u} 1/u \right]/x = \int_{i=1}^{N} \left[\int_{u \in J_x^u} 1/u \right]/x_i = \left[\int_{j=1}^{M_1} 1/u_{1j} \right]/x_1 \cup \ldots \cup \left[\int_{j=1}^{M_N} 1/u_{Nj} \right]/x_N, \tag{5.A}$$

where the simple $\cup$ denotes the union and N is an approach infinity. Note that, the variable x has been divided into N values, and at each of this value u has been divided into M_i values.

Definition 4: Uncertainty in the primary memberships of an IT2 FS $\hat{A}$ consists of a bounded region that we call the footprint of uncertainty (FOU). It is the union of all primary memberships as the following [21-23]:

$$FOU(\hat{A}) = \bigcup_{x \in X} J_x^u . \tag{6.A}$$

Equation (6.A) represents a *vertical-slice of the FOU*, because each of J_x^u is a vertical slice. The shaded region on the xu plane in Fig. 2 is the FOU. If a T2 FS is continuous with a naturally ordered primary variable then the *domain of uncertainty* (DOU) for a T2 FS equal to FOU, i.e., $DOU(\hat{A}) = FOU(\hat{A})$.

Definition 5: The *lower membership function* (LMF) and *upper membership function* (UMF) of $\hat{A}$ are two T1 MFs that bound the DOU. The LMF is associated with the lower bound of $DOU(\hat{A})$ and is denoted by $\underline{\mu}_{\tilde{A}}(x), \forall x \in X$ and the UMF is associated with the upper bound of $DOU(\hat{A})$ and is denoted by $\overline{\mu}_{\tilde{A}}(x), \forall x \in X$, as following:

$$\underline{\mu}_{\tilde{A}}(x) \equiv \underline{DOU(\hat{A})}, \text{ and } \overline{\mu}_{\tilde{A}}(x) \equiv \overline{DOU(\hat{A})}, \qquad \forall x \in X \tag{7.A}$$

We observe that for an IT2 FS $J_x^u = \left[\underline{\mu}_{\tilde{A}}(x), \overline{\mu}_{\tilde{A}}(x) \right], \forall x \in X$. Thus, interval type-2 fuzzy set is denoted by:

$$\hat{A} = \int_{x \in X} \left[\int_{u \in \left[\underline{\mu}_{\tilde{A}}(x), \overline{\mu}_{\tilde{A}}(x) \right] \subseteq [0,1]} 1/u \right]/x . \tag{8.A}$$

Definition 6: For continuous universes of discourse X and U, an embedded IT2 FS has $N \to \infty$ countable-infinity number of elements, where $\hat{A}_E$ contains exactly one element from $J_{x_i}^u$, namely $u_i, (i = 1,2,\ldots)$, each with a secondary degree equal to one, i.e.,

$$\hat{A}_E = \int_{i=1}^{\infty} [1/u_i]/x_i , \ u_i \in J_{x_i}^u \subseteq U = [0,1] \tag{9.A}$$

Set $\hat{A}_E$ is an embedded in $\hat{A}$. There are a countable-infinite number of embedded IT2 FSs for a continuous IT2.

Acknowledgements

The author wishes to thank the reviewers for their excellent suggestions that have been incorporated into this paper. I would like to thank and acknowledge my guides Dr Sanjeev Kumar, and Prof. M.S.Saroa.

IOSR Journal of Computer Engineering (IOSR-JCE)
e-ISSN: 2278-0661,p-ISSN: 2278-8727,
PP 45-57
www.iosrjournals.org

REFERENCES

[1]   J. Castro, O. Castillo, P. Melin, and A. Díaz, Building fuzzy inference systems with a new interval type-2 fuzzy logic toolbox, *Trans. on Computer Science*, 50, 2008, 104–114.

[2]   R. Hndoosh, M.S. Saroa, and S. Kumar, The derivation of interval type-2 fuzzy sets and systems on continuous domain: theory and applications to heart diseases, *International Journal of Science*, 3(10), 2014, 35-54.

[3]   R. Hndoosh, M.S. Saroa, and S. Kumar, Fuzzy mathematical models of type-1 and type-2 for computing the parameters and its applications, *International Journal of Computer Applications*, 104(14), 2014, 17-28.

[4]   N. Karnik, J. Mendel, Centroid of a type-2 fuzzy sets, *An International Journal of Information Sciences*, 132, 2001, 195-220.

[5]   N. Karnik, J. Mendel, Operations on type-2 fuzzy sets, *Fuzzy Sets and Systems*, 122, 2001327–348.

[6]   N. Karnik, J. Mendel, and Q. Liang, (1999), Type-2 fuzzy logic systems, *IEEE Transactions on Fuzzy Systems*, 7(6), 1999, 643-658.

[7]   N. Karnik, J. Mendel, (1998), Introduction to type-2 fuzzy logic systems, *IEEE International Conference on Fuzzy Systems Proceedings*, 1998, 915–920.

[8]   Q. Liang and J. Mendel, Interval type-2 fuzzy logic systems: theory and design," *IEEE Transactions on Fuzzy Systems*, 8(5), 2000, 535–550.

[9]   O. Morales, J. Mendez, and J. Devia, (2012), Centroid of an interval type-2 fuzzy set re-formulation of the problem, *Applied Mathematical Sciences*, 6(122), 2012, 6081-6086.

[10]   J. Mendel, F. Liu, and D. Zhai, α-plane representation for type-2 fuzzy sets: theory and applications, *IEEE Transactions on Fuzzy Systems*, 17(5), 2009, 1189-1207.

[11]   J. Mendel, On answering the question 'Where do i start in order to solve a new problem involving interval type-2 fuzzy sets?'", *International Journal of Information Sciences*, 179, 2009, 3418–3431.

[12]   J. Mendel, type-2 fuzzy sets and systems: an overview, *IEEE computation intelligence magazine*, 2(1), 2007, 20-29.

[13]   J. Mendel, Advances in type-2 fuzzy sets and systems, *International Journal of Information Sciences*, 177, 2007, 84-110.

[14]   J. Mendel, R. John and F. Liu, Interval type-2 fuzzy logic systems made simple, *IEEE Transactions on Fuzzy Systems*, 14(6), 2006, 808-821.

[15]   J. Mendel, Computing derivatives in interval Type-2 fuzzy logic systems, *IEEE Transactions on Fuzzy Systems*, 12(1), 2004, 84-98.

[16]   M. Melgarej, A. Reyes, and A. Garcia (2004), *Computational model and architectural proposal for a hardware type-2 fuzzy system*, (Proc. IEEE FUZZ Conf., Budapest, Hungary, 2004).

[17]   J. Mendel, An architecture for making judgments using computing with words, *International Journal of Applied Mathematics and Computer Science*, 12(3), 2002, 325–335.

[18]   J. Mendel and R. Bob-John, Type-2 fuzzy sets made simple, *IEEE Transactions on Fuzzy Systems*, 10(2), 2002, 117- 127.

[19]   J. Mendel, *Uncertain Rule-Based Fuzzy Logic Systems: Introduction and New Directions* (Prentice-Hall, Upper Saddle River, 2001).

[20]   O. Salazar, H. Serrano and J. Soriano, Centroid of an interval type-2 fuzzy set: continuous vs. discrete, *Ingenieria, Universidad Distrital Francisco José De Caldas*, 16(2), 2011, 67-78.

[21]   D. Wu, J. Mendel, and S. Coupland, (2012), Enhanced interval approach for encoding words into interval type-2 fuzzy sets and its convergence analysis, *IEEE Transactions on Fuzzy Systems*, 20(3), 2012, 499-513.

[22]   H. Wu and J. Mendel, Classification of battlefield ground vehicles using acoustic features and fuzzy logic rule-based classifiers, *IEEE Trans. Fuzzy Syst.*, 15(1), 2007, pp. 56–72.

[23]   H. Wu and J. Mendel, Uncertainty bounds and their use in the design of interval type-2 fuzzy logic systems, *IEEE Transactions on Fuzzy Systems*, 10(5), 2002, 622-639.

[24]   J. Zeng, L. Xie, Z. Liu, Type-2 fuzzy Gaussian mixture models, *Journal of the Pattern Recognition Society*, 41, 2008, 3636 – 3643.